HOPE FULL

Hope Full

Lisa Wood

ISBN (Paperback): 979-8-218-79293-0

ISBN (eBook): 979-8-218-79294-7

Printed in the United States of America

First Edition, 2025

Cover design by Stilwell Design Solutions

Published by Lisa Wood

Contents

Dedication   vii

Introduction   viii

About the Author   ix

1   The Silence of Suffering   1

2   Seeds of Motherhood   6

3   The Wounds We Carry   11

4   Losses Within Losses   16

5   The Fragile Hope   20

6   Silent Pain, Loud Lies   25

7   Second Chances, Same Grief   29

8   A Church That Restores Hope   37

9   God's Timing, My Pain   42

10 A Mother's Praise   48

11 A Vision of Hope   53

12 The Impossible Path   59

13 Twists and Turns   64

14 A Double Portion   69

15 Behind the Promise   75

16 Labor of Love   80

17 Naming the Promise   85

18 For the One Who Still Waits   90

Final Prayer   95

Acknowledgments   97

Devotional Appendix   99

Declarations of Hope   102

Practical Prayer Strategy   104

Stay Connected   106

Dedication

To Jason and Consuelo Murrell —

The selfless, faithful couple who carried our miracle with grace, courage, and unwavering love.

Your obedience to God's voice, your generosity of spirit, and your willingness to walk this sacred journey with us brought our sons into the world and into our arms. There are no words strong enough to express our gratitude, but this book is a small offering of the legacy your sacrifice helped create.

Because of you, we are a family.

With love, honor, and eternal thanks.

Introduction

If you've picked up this book, there's a good chance your heart is aching.

Maybe you've experienced a miscarriage. Maybe you've walked the long, lonely road of infertility. Maybe someone you love is hurting, and you're trying to understand how to be there for them. Wherever you find yourself today, I want you to know something right from the beginning:

You are not alone.

This is not just a story about pain — it's a story about **God's presence** in the middle of it. It's about **grief, confusion**, and **faith that wavers**... but also about a God who never does. It's about **a woman who broke**, but who was never beyond God's ability to heal.

This is my story. It's raw. It's honest. But more than anything, it's filled with hope — even when I didn't always feel it. And if you'll walk with me through the chapters ahead, I believe God will meet you in your story too.

You may not know what's next. But you're not forgotten. And you are not without hope.

Hebrews 10:23 (NLT) "Let us hold tightly without wavering to the hope we affirm, for God can be trusted to keep his promise."

About the Author

Lisa Wood is a wife, mother, and passionate follower of Jesus whose journey through infertility and miscarriage has shaped her heart for ministering to the brokenhearted. Her story is one of loss, surrender, and God's miraculous redemption — and she shares it with raw honesty and unwavering hope.

Lisa has spent years encouraging women facing silent battles, reminding them that their story isn't over and that God is still faithful. She lives in Kentucky with her husband Chris and their three sons — Christopher, Matthias, and Israel — living proof of God's goodness and perfect timing.

Hope Full is her debut book and a deeply personal offering to anyone who has ever questioned God's plan while longing for a miracle.

1

The Silence of Suffering

Scripture: *"The Lord is close to the brokenhearted and saves those who are crushed in spirit."* — Psalm 34:18 (NIV)

My first miscarriage left me feeling achingly alone. I carried not only the loss of a baby, but also the heavy weight of shame. I was embarrassed to talk about it, afraid of what others might think. In my mind, I kept hearing accusations: *You're not enough. You're defective. This is your fault.*

Very quickly, I realized most people didn't know how to respond. They were uncomfortable, unsure of what to say, and often chose silence instead. That silence cut deeply. It made me feel like miscarriage was a subject too taboo to touch, leaving me to believe I had to hide my grief. Pretending everything was okay became my mask, even while my heart was breaking.

I didn't know how to grieve this type of loss, and no one seemed able to guide me through it. Looking back, I can see that the silence around my pain made the recovery process even harder.

When God first instructed me to share my story, I resisted. Vulnerability terrified me. But God knew what I didn't yet understand

— that my story could become a lifeline for others. That it could give women permission to speak out, to ask for help, and to discover that they aren't walking through this valley alone.

For me, healing began with writing. I didn't stand up in church and tell everyone right away — I started in the privacy of my journal. Putting my grief into words, even when no one else saw it, opened the door for God to meet me in those raw places. That step of honesty with Him prepared me to one day be honest with others.

If you've ever felt like your grief was "too much" for others — too awkward, too painful, too heavy — I want you to know this: you are not alone. Others have walked this road. And most importantly, there is a God who draws near to the brokenhearted.

Healing often begins with small, intentional steps: bringing your grief to God in prayer, letting Scripture speak truth over the lies, and refusing to carry the weight in silence. You don't have to have all the answers to start — you just have to take the first step.

This journey won't be easy to read. It hasn't been easy to write. But I believe it will be worth it. My prayer is that those of you who have experienced miscarriage will find comfort here, and those walking through infertility will find hope. God is no respecter of persons. What He has done for me, He can and will do for you.

Steps Toward Hope

Silence may feel like the safest place to hide your grief, but silence can deepen the wound. For me, the first shift came when I dared to bring my raw honesty to God. My prayers weren't polished — many were just tears — but He met me there. If all you can do is whisper His name or say, "God, I need You," that's enough. He isn't waiting for eloquence; He's waiting for honesty.

Over time, I also learned to let one trusted person into my story. At first, it was just a sentence, nothing more: "I've been through a miscarriage." Saying it out loud was terrifying, but each time I shared, the weight grew a little lighter. If you are carrying your grief in silence, you don't have to share everything all at once. Start small. Tell God first, then someone who will listen without judgment.

And finally, give yourself a rhythm of comfort. For me, it was playing worship music, writing prayers in a journal, or taking a walk when the heaviness threatened to suffocate me. These weren't grand gestures — just tiny ways to breathe again. Little by little, they reminded me that I wasn't as alone as I felt.

Healing doesn't happen overnight, but each small step toward openness — with God, with others, and even with yourself — makes space for hope to rise.

Reflection Questions:

1. Have you ever experienced a grief you felt you couldn't talk about?
2. In what ways have you tried to hide or downplay your pain?
3. How would it feel to bring that pain into the light — to God or to a trusted person?

Journaling Prompt: Write a letter to God expressing your silent grief. Don't worry about sounding "right." Just be honest. Let Him into the places you've tried to carry alone.

Your Reflections
Use this space to write your thoughts, prayers, or reflections as
God speaks to your heart.

2

Seeds of Motherhood

Scripture: *"Before I formed you in the womb I knew you, before you were born I set you apart."* — Jeremiah 1:5 (NIV)

The very first gift I remember receiving was a pink baby doll. I must have been only three or four years old, but I still remember how much that doll meant to me. Out of all the toys I had, it was the one I cherished most. I may not have felt anything "maternal" at that age, but I know I loved that doll deeply. Looking back, I see it as the first hint of something God had planted inside me — a longing to nurture.

As I grew, my collection of dolls grew with me. I treated them as though they were real babies. I had cribs, cradles, strollers, high chairs, and even a dresser drawer filled with tiny clothes. One corner of my bedroom was dedicated entirely to my little nursery. While many girls my age were moving on to makeup and boys, I was still "mothering" my dolls. It wasn't just pretend play to me — it felt like who I was.

I was also blessed to grow up in church. I always had some awareness of God and the importance of living right. The church I attended didn't provide much depth in teaching, but it gave me a foundation — a basic sense of right and wrong. I accepted Jesus into my heart at a young age, though I didn't yet understand what it meant to walk with Him daily. That understanding would come later, through seasons of struggle, surrender, and ultimately, dependence on Him.

Now, when I look back, I see how intentional God was from the very beginning. That longing to mother wasn't random. It wasn't immaturity or weakness. It was a seed of purpose — one He Himself planted in me. And while that seed would later be tested and pressed through years of waiting, grief, and loss, God never let it die.

It took me a long time to realize I even needed to bring those longings to God — and even longer to understand how. For years, I carried them silently, unsure of what to say or afraid of being disappointed. But one of the most healing shifts I made was learning that I didn't have to have polished words or the perfect prayer. I just had to bring Him what was real. My encouragement to you is this: don't wait until it feels like the "right time." Don't wait until you feel strong enough or spiritual enough. Start now. Take those longings — even the raw, messy ones — and place them in His hands.

To the woman reading this who has always wanted to be a mother: I want you to hear me clearly. That desire in your heart matters. God sees it. He placed it there. And no matter what your journey has looked like — or how long it has been — it is not something to be ashamed of or to bury.

Seeds often go through a season of darkness before they break through the soil. But they are never forgotten by the One who planted them. Holding onto that truth can be one of the first steps toward healing — trusting that what God plants, He intends to bring to life.

Steps Toward Hope:

It took me a long time to realize that the desires planted in my heart — like the longing for motherhood — were not weaknesses or flaws. For years, I pushed them down, afraid of what they meant or ashamed that they hadn't yet been fulfilled. But burying them only made me feel more alone.

What shifted everything was learning to bring those longings to God — not polished, not "safe," but in all their rawness. Sometimes that meant sitting quietly and saying, "Lord, this hurts, but I still want to trust You." Other times it was journaling my dreams, even when I wasn't sure if they would ever come true.

If you carry a longing that feels too heavy to speak out loud, I want to encourage you: don't wait for the "perfect" moment to bring it before Him. Start now, just as you are. God placed that seed in your heart, and He isn't surprised by the ache it carries. He is faithful to tend what He plants, even when the soil looks dry.

Hope grows when we dare to bring our deepest desires into His light, and trust that He knows the right time for them to bloom.

Reflection Questions:

1. What early desires or dreams did God plant in your heart?
2. Have you ever dismissed them as childish, unimportant, or unrealistic?
3. What fears keep you from bringing those longings to God openly?
4. What would it look like to start practicing that *today* instead of waiting for the "right" time?

Journaling Prompt:

Write about your earliest memories of wanting to nurture, protect, or care for others. Then, turn those memories into a prayer — even if it feels raw or incomplete. Simply tell God, "This is my heart. I give it to You."

Your Reflections
Use this space to write your thoughts, prayers, or reflections as God speaks to your heart.

3

The Wounds We Carry

Scripture: *"Therefore, there is now no condemnation for those who are in Christ Jesus."* — Romans 8:1 (NIV)

As a young girl, I became a victim of molestation at the hands of a family member. The pain of that betrayal left a wound that lingered for years — not just physically, but emotionally and spiritually. Sadly, that was only the beginning. A few years later, I was violated again through sexual assault.

In between those traumas, I endured relentless bullying in middle school — treated as an outsider, mocked, and made to feel like I didn't belong anywhere. Later, as a teenager, I became trapped in an abusive relationship that stripped away what little confidence I had left. Each violation reinforced the same poisonous lie: that I was worthless, broken, and beyond repair.

What made it even harder was that I didn't feel safe enough to speak up. Like many girls in similar situations, I convinced myself that it must have been my fault. That shame rooted itself deep inside me, feeding lies about my worth and identity. It shaped how I saw myself, my body, and my ability to be loved. Before I even had a chance to discover who I truly was, that understanding was already fractured.

As I entered adolescence, the wound became a filter through which I saw everything. I struggled with self-esteem and boundaries. I longed for love but didn't believe I deserved it. Out of that brokenness, I made choices that I thought would fill the emptiness — but those choices only deepened it. And though I didn't know it then, some of those decisions would later carry physical consequences that impacted my fertility. What began as wounds to my heart eventually touched my body, shaping the very path of motherhood I longed for.

Looking back, I can see how the enemy tried to convince me I was disqualified — from love, from motherhood, from God's best. He used every trauma to plant seeds of shame and defeat, hoping I would never dare believe for healing or redemption. But God, in His mercy, never left me. Even when I didn't know how to cry out, He was present. Even when I thought my future as a mother was lost, He had already written a different ending to my story.

Through time, prayer, and God's healing hand, I've come to understand something life-changing: I was never what was done to me. I was always God's daughter. Chosen. Loved. Worthy. And so are you.

If you've experienced trauma — whether anyone else knows about it or not — I want you to know that healing is possible. Your pain does not disqualify you from purpose, from love, or from motherhood. No matter how damaged you feel, God still sees the whole you — the healed you — that He created from the very beginning.

STEPS TOWARD HOPE

For a long time, I believed the wounds of my past defined me. Abuse, bullying, broken relationships — they all left marks that felt permanent. I carried shame like it was stitched into my skin. What began to change me was realizing that silence only kept the wound open, but honesty — even whispered honesty before God — made room for healing.

Healing didn't come overnight. It came in layers, in moments where I dared to tell God the truth about how broken I felt. It came when I shared small pieces of my story with trusted people who reminded me I was not what had been done to me. Slowly, truth began to take the place of lies.

If you've carried hidden wounds, you don't have to wait until you feel strong to begin healing. Start by inviting God into one small corner of the pain. You may not know what to say, but even "Lord, help me here" is enough. Every step toward honesty opens a door for Him to show you that you are more than what happened to you — you are His daughter, loved and whole in His eyes.

Reflection Questions:

1. Are there wounds from your past that you've never fully acknowledged or spoken aloud?
2. What lies did pain or trauma cause you to believe about yourself?
3. Which Scriptures could you use to replace those lies with truth?
4. What would it look like to invite God into one of your most painful memories?

Journaling Prompt:

Write a letter to your younger self — the version of you who was wounded. What does she need to hear from you today? What does she need to hear from God?

Your Reflections
Use this space to write your thoughts, prayers, or reflections as God speaks to your heart.

4

Losses Within Losses

Scripture: *"...to bestow on them a crown of beauty instead of ashes..."* — Isaiah 61:3 (NIV)

Most of my adolescent and teen years were marked by pain. The trauma I carried from childhood made it hard to cope with everyday life. I struggled to concentrate in school, often feeling lost and emotionally overwhelmed. Eventually, I stopped going to class altogether and had to finish high school in night classes to graduate. The failure to walk the graduation stage with my peers seemed to confirm every lie I already believed about myself: that I was broken, unworthy, and destined to disappoint.

Around that same time, my sister Holly passed away unexpectedly. She wasn't just my sister — she was my very best friend, my safe place, the one I could always turn to no matter what I was facing. Holly had a way of lifting me up without minimizing my pain, of encouraging me while still holding me accountable. Losing her felt like losing my anchor. Her death was a blow I didn't know how to recover from. The grief was suffocating. I had already been drowning emotionally, and now I was completely submerged. With the person I trusted most suddenly gone, I was spiraling — desperate to find anything that might numb the ache. In that desperation, I rushed into marriage. Not out of love, but out of a longing to escape. I thought if I could just start over, things would change. But pain doesn't disappear when you change your surroundings. If it's not healed, it follows you. And that's exactly what happened. That relationship wasn't grounded in God or in truth. It was built on brokenness trying to fix brokenness.

Looking back, I can see now that what I was really searching for was control. Life had felt so unpredictable, so full of loss, and I thought maybe if I could create something stable — even if it wasn't healthy — I could finally feel safe. But the safety I found was false, and the consequences were real.

Even then, God never turned His back on me. He was with me in the mess, even when I didn't know how to look for Him. That chapter of my life was dark, but He never stopped holding the pen. And even though I couldn't see it at the time, He was already preparing beauty from my ashes.

Steps Toward Hope:

After Holly's death, I tried to run from grief. I thought if I just changed my circumstances, the pain would stay behind. But grief is not something you can outrun. It follows until it is faced. What began to shift for me was giving myself permission to stop running — to sit with God and name the losses I had buried.

That practice didn't erase the ache, but it lightened the weight. I learned that grief can exist alongside hope. The tears didn't mean I lacked faith — they meant I was human. And in those tears, God met me.

If you're tempted to escape your pain — through busyness, through relationships, through distraction — I encourage you to pause instead. Sit with God and tell Him what hurts. Say the words you're afraid to admit: "I miss her." "This feels unfair." "I don't know how to keep going." He is not offended by your honesty. He welcomes it.

Healing doesn't mean forgetting. It means letting God carry what is too heavy for you. And slowly, He will show you beauty even in the ashes.

Reflection Questions:

1. Have you ever made a decision from a place of grief or fear?
2. How have past losses impacted the way you view your future?
3. Where can you see God's hand — even in the chapters of your life that feel like ashes?

Journaling Prompt: Write about a season where you felt like your life was falling apart. What comfort would you offer to your younger self now, knowing what God has brought you through?

Your Reflections
Use this space to write your thoughts, prayers, or reflections as
God speaks to your heart.

_____

_____

_____

_____

_____

_____

_____

_____

_____

_____

_____

_____

_____

5

The Fragile Hope

Scripture: *"Trust in the Lord with all your heart and lean not on your own understanding."* — Proverbs 3:5 (NIV)

Two weeks after we were married, I made an appointment at the free clinic. All I cared about was finding out if pregnancy was even possible for me. I had never been to a gynecologist before and had no idea what to expect. When the doctor finished the exam, I asked him only one question: *"Is there anything you can see that would prevent me from becoming pregnant?"*

I know he must have thought I was out of my mind. I was 18, newly married, and the only thing on my heart was whether or not I could bring a child into this world. What was I thinking? In my young and desperate heart, motherhood felt like the one thing that could make me whole.

Eventually, I did become pregnant. The moment I saw that positive test, my heart leapt. For a brief time, I let myself dream of the future: a crib in the corner, a baby in my arms, a family beginning to grow. But within the first couple of weeks, joy gave way to cramping and spotting.

My doctor told me quickly that I was experiencing a miscarriage. No tests. No explanations. He simply prescribed medication meant to convince my body it was time for my period and to expel the pregnancy. What followed was unimaginable pain — not only physically, but emotionally and spiritually.

At the time, I had no framework for what was happening. I didn't know how to ask questions or advocate for myself. I trusted the doctor's authority without hesitation, and in the silence, I carried the lie that I was defective. What I didn't realize until years later is that being uninformed doesn't make the loss any less real. That was my baby, and I was losing that child.

Grief came in waves, but it was a strange kind of grief. Part of me wanted to deny it altogether. If I could convince myself it had all been a mistake — that maybe I hadn't really been pregnant — then I didn't have to face the permanence of loss. Denial was easier to carry than truth, because truth felt too heavy. Too final.

This was the first time I began to realize how fragile hope could be — and how fiercely it needed to be protected. One moment, I was imagining baby names and lullabies; the next, I was staring into emptiness. I wanted so badly to believe I could still become a mother, but fear and confusion wrapped around me like chains. My mind became a battlefield of "what ifs" and accusations: *What if I had done something wrong? What if my body was broken? What if this would always be my story?*

Looking back now, I see that I wasn't fighting the way God calls us to fight our battles. Instead of running to Him, I let fear, shame, and silence become my weapons — weapons that only wounded me further. I didn't cry out to the God who comforts. I didn't anchor myself in His promises. I didn't invite Him into my grief. I tried to carry it all alone, and it nearly crushed me.

And yet — He never left me. Even in my numbness and confusion, He was there. He saw me curled up in pain, both in body and heart. He heard the questions I couldn't even form. He held onto me when I didn't know how to hold onto Him.

In hindsight, I can see that God was beginning to teach me something in that valley of loss. He was showing me that my trust couldn't rest on outcomes, or on doctors, or on my own fragile expectations. He was whispering that real hope would require surrender, and that the battle for motherhood wasn't one I could win in my own strength.

That miscarriage was not the end of my story. It was the beginning of my understanding: that grief is real, that hope is fragile, but that God's presence is constant.

STEPS TOWARD HOPE

When I lost my first baby, I carried so much confusion. I trusted the doctor without question, and when it was over, I tried to minimize the grief — telling myself maybe it hadn't really been a pregnancy, maybe it didn't matter. But denial didn't bring healing. It only deepened the ache.

What helped me begin moving forward was admitting the truth: that was my baby, and losing that life was real. Saying it aloud gave me permission to grieve what I had tried to dismiss. And when I brought that truth to God, I discovered that He was not pushing me away in disappointment — He was drawing me closer in compassion.

If you're struggling with fragile hope, don't be afraid to speak the truth of your loss. Let yourself grieve what was real. And as you do, trust that God's presence is not fragile — it will not break under the weight of your questions or your tears. Hope may feel delicate right now, but in His hands, it is unshakable.

Reflection Questions:

1. Have you ever ignored your own instincts because someone "in authority" told you otherwise?
2. What does it mean to you to trust God when things don't make sense?
3. In what ways has your hope been tested — and protected — through loss?

Journaling Prompt: Write a prayer to God expressing the hopes you're afraid to speak out loud. Ask Him to strengthen your trust and help you see His hand even when clarity is lacking.

Your Reflections
Use this space to write your thoughts, prayers, or reflections as
God speaks to your heart.

6

Silent Pain, Loud Lies

Scripture: *"The thief comes only to steal and kill and destroy; I have come that they may have life, and have it to the full."* — John 10:10 (NIV)

There was a season when my pain became invisible — not because it didn't hurt, but because I learned how to hide it. On the outside, I was functioning: smiling when expected, performing when needed. But inside, I was unraveling.

About a year after my first miscarriage, I had another experience. I never officially confirmed that I was pregnant, but I knew something wasn't right. I hadn't had a period in some time (my cycle was irregular, so I couldn't say exactly how long). Then came the same pain, the same spotting. After a few days, I passed a mass that I knew was not "normal."

Once again, I suffered in silence. I told absolutely no one. Shame and anger closed me off. I asked myself, *Who would understand? Who would support me? Who wouldn't blame me?* So I minimized it: *It's not that bad. I'll just keep going.* But ignoring pain doesn't heal it. It only buries it deeper.

The lies I believed in that season were deafening: *This is your fault. You're broken. You're being punished. You don't deserve to be a mother.* Those lies began to shape everything: how I saw myself, how I related to others, even how I related to God. They cost me my marriage. And they built a wall between me and the Lord — not because He had moved, but because I had stopped bringing Him my truth.

It took time, and so much grace, to begin recognizing those thoughts for what they were: attacks from the enemy meant to steal my joy and hope. The more I hid my grief, the more power it had over me. But when I finally began to speak it aloud — to name the loss and confront the lies — God began to meet me with truth.

Pain loses its grip in the presence of truth. And God's truth is always life-giving.

STEPS TOWARD HOPE

The silence I carried after that second loss nearly consumed me. I convinced myself no one would understand, that my pain would only be met with judgment or dismissal. But the truth was, hiding it gave the lies more power. Every time I stayed quiet, the enemy's voice grew louder: *You're broken. You're being punished. You don't deserve to be a mother.*

Hope began to return when I broke that silence. First with God — simply saying, "This hurts, and I don't know how to carry it." Then, slowly, with trusted people who could sit with me in the pain without turning away.

If you've been keeping your losses locked inside, I want to encourage you: the enemy thrives in silence, but truth flourishes in the light. Speaking your grief doesn't make it heavier — it makes it shareable. And when you share it with God, He replaces the lies with His truth: *You are loved. You are chosen. You are not disqualified.*

Reflection Questions:

1. Are there any losses or wounds you've kept silent about?
2. What lies have you believed about yourself or your worth?
3. What does it look like to invite God into your pain — not after you've healed, but in the middle of it?

Journaling Prompt: Write out a list of lies you've believed about your identity or your situation. Then, write God's truth next to each one. Speak His truth over yourself, even if you're still learning to believe it.

Your Reflections
Use this space to write your thoughts, prayers, or reflections as
God speaks to your heart.

_____

_____

_____

_____

_____

_____

_____

_____

_____

_____

_____

_____

_____

7

Second Chances, Same Grief

Scripture: *"Even though I walk through the darkest valley, I will fear no evil, for you are with me."* — Psalm 23:4 (NIV)

When I first met Chris, it wasn't in church or through mutual friends walking closely with God. We met on the dance floor of a nightclub — two people carrying heavy baggage and looking for something to fill the emptiness inside. He was fun, attentive, and made me feel like I mattered. At that point in my life, I was so desperate to be seen that his attention felt like oxygen.

We moved in together quickly, believing companionship could patch over the cracks in our hearts. But the truth was, our relationship wasn't grounded at all. It was built on shaky foundations — long nights, quick thrills, and the illusion that love meant simply not being alone. We argued, avoided hard truths, and numbed pain instead of facing it. Deep down, I knew we were building on sand, but I didn't yet know how to build differently.

Over time, though, God began to stir something in both of us. It wasn't one single turning point, but a series of small shifts

— convictions we couldn't ignore, hard conversations we couldn't avoid, realizations that if we wanted this to last, it couldn't stay the way it was. Slowly, we began lowering our walls. We became more honest — not just about our pasts, but about our fears and hopes for the future.

When we finally invited God into the center of our relationship, everything began to change. The things that once pulled us apart started drawing us closer together. Arguments turned into opportunities for growth. Our love deepened, no longer just about survival or attention, but about trust and commitment.

Looking back now, the contrast is striking. What began in brokenness on a nightclub dance floor became, through years of hard work and God's grace, a love that was real, tested, and strong. For the first time in a long time, I allowed myself to believe that maybe, just maybe, God had a new chapter for me.

When Chris and I married, I didn't just gain a husband — I also became a mother in a new way. Christopher, his little boy, was only three years old when we met, and from the very beginning I loved him as my own. Being part of his life brought both joy and responsibility. It wasn't always easy stepping into motherhood through a blended family, but it was real, and it was sacred. God was showing me that motherhood comes in many forms, and that His plan for family is often wider and deeper than we first imagine. Christopher became a living reminder that even in the midst of loss and longing, God was already entrusting me with the gift of raising a son.

But before we even reached the altar, that hope was tested. Just months before our wedding day, while Chris and I were trying to get our lives on track and prepare for marriage, I went to the doctor because I had been spotting for two weeks. At that appointment, I learned I was pregnant. Instead of joy, tears of despair filled my eyes. Deep down, I already believed something was wrong. The spotting had convinced me this pregnancy would not last, and any flicker of hope that tried to rise up, I quickly pushed back down.

The doctor ordered bloodwork and had me return 48 hours later. The second test confirmed what I feared — the pregnancy was not viable. Hearing those words made the loss real in a way I had tried to avoid.

On the phone with the doctor, I whispered through tears, *"What do I do? You tell me — I'm trusting you."* He explained that the safest course was to schedule a D&C since the bleeding had gone on so long. He assured me it would clear out what remained and protect my health.

Chris and I agreed. It was New Year's Eve, December 31, 2003. While the world celebrated fresh beginnings, I was being checked into a hospital to say goodbye to a dream. The timing felt cruel.

By the time they took me back, I was so distraught that my body physically resisted. My veins retracted. Normally IVs were simple, but that day, after ten failed attempts — arms, hands, even my foot — they still couldn't get access. Finally, the staff wrapped my arms in warm blankets to coax the veins back. I was wheeled into the operating room trembling, exhausted, and emotionally numb. The anesthesiologist numbed my hand, found a vein, and within moments, the medication took over.

When I woke up, Chris was sitting beside me, holding my hand. The doctor had already left, leaving instructions with the nurse. I was to return in a few days for bloodwork to confirm everything was back to normal. Groggy and overwhelmed, I followed orders and went home, trying to convince myself this nightmare was behind me.

But the grief was only beginning. When I returned for the follow-up, my bloodwork showed pregnancy hormones were still present. Confusion doesn't begin to describe what I felt. Scared. Frustrated. Angry. Hadn't the D&C resolved this? Why hadn't my doctor known?

Chris wasn't with me this time. We had assumed it was routine, and he had already missed work to care for me. The doctor recommended Methotrexate, administered by injection. Something in me wanted to press harder for answers. I asked about an ultrasound, saying it would give me peace of mind. He brushed me off, insisting it wasn't necessary. With confidence, he assured me this was the best course of action. I was young, naïve, and desperate to trust someone. So I agreed.

Within hours, I was doubled over in unbearable pain. Chris rushed me to the hospital. By the time we arrived, I could barely stand. The truth came quickly: the pregnancy had been ectopic. Life had been growing in the wrong place — my fallopian tube — and it had ruptured. Blood filled my abdomen. My body was shutting down. The pain was indescribable.

Everything moved fast. Emergency surgery. Shock. The doctor wasn't sure she could save my fallopian tube. As I was rushed to the operating room, I wondered if this was the end of my chance to ever become a mother.

Looking back, I realize how close I came to losing my life — all because a simple ultrasound had been dismissed. If my doctor had listened to my concerns and checked more thoroughly, the rupture might have been caught before it nearly destroyed me.

That's why I share this with such urgency: you must advocate for yourself. Even if you feel young, inexperienced, or intimidated, your voice matters. Ask for an ultrasound. Ask for the tests. Don't settle for shortcuts. Doctors are human. They can overlook things, take the easy route, or dismiss concerns. But this is your body, your health, your future. You have every right to demand clarity and care.

The surgery was grueling, but by God's grace, the surgeon spent hours carefully repairing my fallopian tube. She knew how desperately I wanted to be a mother and did everything possible to preserve that hope. I see God's hand in that — guiding her, sustaining me, protecting my future even when I couldn't see it.

That experience was the most terrifying and faith-shaking of my life. But it also became the one that drew me closest to Him. I was broken — body, mind, and spirit — but I was not abandoned. God never left me on that operating table. He never left me in the aftermath of grief. And even though I couldn't yet see how He would redeem it, I knew He was near.

Steps Toward Hope

That season taught me something I wish I had known much earlier: silence and surrender are not the same thing. For years, I stayed quiet — out of fear, shame, or intimidation — and in that silence I nearly lost my life. But when I finally learned what surrender really was, everything began to shift.

Surrender didn't mean I stopped caring or fighting for answers. It meant I stopped carrying the weight alone. For me, it looked like bringing God the whole messy truth — the fear, the questions, the confusion — and trusting that He could hold it all without turning away. And it also looked like finding my voice with doctors, refusing to shrink back when something didn't feel right, and learning to advocate for myself without apology.

That combination — raw honesty before God and courage to speak up for myself — became one of the greatest acts of faith I have ever practiced. It was how I said, *"Lord, I trust You with my life, and I will also steward this life You've given me."*

If you are in a season where grief and fear feel overwhelming, let Him into the places you've been hiding. Tell Him the truth about what hurts and what scares you. He can handle your honesty. And as you do, don't be afraid to use the voice He gave you — to ask questions, to seek help, to fight for your health and your hope.

I had to come to the edge of losing everything to realize this: silence was never my protection. But surrender — full, honest surrender — became the very place I discovered God's nearness like never before.

If you've walked through trauma and feel paralyzed by what might come next, you don't have to leap into tomorrow with forced bravery. Start with surrender today. Tell God your fear. Hand Him your questions. And trust that He can hold both your longing and your trembling heart at the same time. Hope doesn't erase fear — but God's presence makes it possible to keep moving, even with fear still in the room.

REFLECTION QUESTIONS

1. Have you ever experienced a loss that came so quickly it felt like whiplash?
2. How did God show up for you in a time of emergency or trauma?
3. What does it mean to hold both grief and gratitude in the same hand?

JOURNALING PROMPT

Write about a time you felt completely out of control — and how God met you there. Even if healing is still in progress, where can you see His fingerprints?

Your Reflections
Use this space to write your thoughts, prayers, or reflections as
God speaks to your heart.

_____

_____

_____

_____

_____

_____

_____

_____

_____

_____

_____

_____

8

A Church That Restores Hope

SCRIPTURE: *"CAST ALL YOUR ANXIETY ON HIM BECAUSE HE CARES FOR YOU."* — 1 PETER 5:7 (NIV)

After all I had been through, I didn't expect to find healing in church. My past experiences had left me wary of religious spaces that emphasized performance over presence. But when Chris and I began working to bring God into our relationship, He led us to **Abounding Grace** in New York — the very place where we were already living.

That church family became a refuge. They surrounded us during some of the darkest moments of loss. They didn't judge us. They didn't condemn us. They simply opened their arms, prayed with us, and walked beside us when our faith was fragile. They gave us space to grieve while reminding us that God still loved us. Looking back, I see Abounding Grace as God's gift of mercy — a covering when we could barely keep standing. It wasn't just a church we attended; it was the safe place God used to begin rebuilding our faith.

But eventually, God led us back to Kentucky. Returning home placed us right where He wanted us — at **Abundant Life Church**. This was not just a move across states; it was a return to the spiritual soil where God had planted His name for me and my family. And it was there, in that house, that my hope was finally restored.

Abundant Life embraced us — not despite our story, but because of it. They didn't demand perfection; they offered presence. When we shared our desire to start a family, they prayed with us. When discouragement threatened to overwhelm, they stood with us. When we began to explore new paths to parenthood, they became our loudest cheerleaders.

Most importantly, they didn't try to carry my burdens for me. Instead, they taught me to **cast them at the feet of Jesus**, just as Scripture commands: *"Cast all your anxiety on Him because He cares for you"* (1 Peter 5:7). They reminded me that only He could shoulder the weight of my grief and longing. Psalm 55:22 became an anchor for my weary heart: *"Cast your burden on the Lord, and He will sustain you; He will never permit the righteous to be moved."*

God often heals through His people. He doesn't only speak from heaven — He speaks through community, through hugs, through prayers whispered in the hallway. Abounding Grace helped us take our first steps of faith together as a couple, and Abundant Life taught us how to plant ourselves deeply in Christ. Both were part of God's plan to lead us from survival to restoration.

If you don't have a church home, I encourage you to find one that preaches the uncompromised Word of God and points you back to Jesus as your ultimate source of strength. The right church won't try to replace Him — they'll help you see Him more clearly.

STEPS TOWARD HOPE

I didn't realize how deeply I needed community until I found myself in the middle of it. Both Abounding Grace and Abundant Life became places where my pain was met with prayer, where my doubts were met with encouragement, and where my brokenness was not hidden but held. Their presence reminded me that God doesn't just comfort from heaven — He comforts through His people.

If you've been walking through loss alone, I gently encourage you to take a step toward community. It may feel risky, especially if you've been hurt by people or by the church before. But the right community doesn't add weight to your grief — it helps carry it.

Healing doesn't happen in isolation. It happens when we let others stand with us, pray with us, and remind us of God's truth when our own hearts are too tired to remember. You don't have to find a perfect church — you just need a place where you can be real and where Jesus is at the center.

Reflection Questions:

1. Have you ever hesitated to step into community out of
    fear of being misunderstood?
2. What would a "small first step" toward healing commu-
    nity look like for you right now?
3. How might God be inviting you to let others walk with
    you in this season, even in simple ways?

Journaling Prompt: Reflect on a time when someone's presence — not their advice — brought you comfort. How did God
use them to speak love or truth into your life?

Your Reflections
Use this space to write your thoughts, prayers, or reflections as
God speaks to your heart.

_____

_____

_____

_____

_____

_____

_____

_____

_____

_____

_____

_____

9

God's Timing, My Pain

Scripture: *"He has made everything beautiful in its time. He has also set eternity in the human heart; yet no one can fathom what God has done from beginning to end."* — Ecclesiastes 3:11 (NIV)

After our wedding, I was eager to try again — eager for motherhood, for new beginnings, for hope realized. But I was also impatient. I had waited so long and experienced so much loss that I just wanted something, anything, to finally go right.

So when I was prescribed Clomid to help with ovulation, I took it without hesitation. I prayed, but I didn't wait to hear God's answer. Deep down, I felt a nudge to hold off, to trust His timing, but I dismissed it. I told myself this was my chance, and I didn't want to miss it.

The first round came and went without success. No pregnancy. No breakthrough. Just more waiting. The disappointment stung. By the second round, my doctor suggested doubling the dosage. That's when God's voice became unmistakable: *"Do not take that medicine."*

It wasn't a vague impression — it was clear. But instead of obeying, I argued with Him in my heart. *Why not me, Lord? Why do I have to keep waiting while everyone else gets their miracle? Isn't this finally my time?* I let my longing speak louder than His voice.

And so, I took it anyway.

That decision led to a pregnancy — one that filled me with both joy and fear. For the first time, I made it through the fragile first trimester. Each milestone felt like proof that maybe this time it would be different. I dreamed of names and nursery colors. I imagined what it would be like to hold my child. I prayed over my womb, thanking God for this gift. Slowly, I let myself hope.

At 18 weeks, we went in for an ultrasound, expecting to find out if we were having a son or a daughter. Chris and I walked into that appointment with excitement, and Christopher came too, eager to learn whether he'd be welcoming a brother or a sister. But instead of joyful news, the technician told us they couldn't confirm everything yet — we would need to come back for another scan at 20 weeks.

Those two weeks felt like an eternity. I carried both anticipation and unease, clinging to fragile hope while fighting back fear. I prayed. I tried to stay positive. I told myself that at the next appointment, we would get the answers we were waiting for.

At 20 weeks, we returned for the follow-up ultrasound, expecting clarity and closure to the questions left at 18 weeks. Chris sat beside me, Christopher close by, the room still filled with the anticipation we had carried for those two long weeks. I wanted so badly to believe this would be the day we found out if we were having a boy or a girl — the day joy would finally replace all my fear.

But as the technician pressed the probe to my stomach, the silence in the room was deafening. She searched. She shifted. She pressed again. My heart pounded as I watched her face, praying to see a smile or hear words of reassurance. Instead, her eyes grew serious, and she quietly excused herself to get the doctor.

In that moment, the world seemed to stop. The walls felt like they were closing in. My body, which had been carrying life, suddenly felt like a tomb. When the doctor finally spoke the words, *"I'm sorry, there's no heartbeat,"* it was as if the floor dropped out from under me.

Shock gave way to sobs that seemed to rise from the deepest part of my soul. My whole body shook as I clutched my stomach, instinctively holding onto the child I knew I would never get to raise. I felt helpless. Betrayed by my body. Crushed under the weight of dreams that would never be realized.

Chris held me tightly, his tears falling silently, while Christopher sat confused and heartbroken beside us. I had no words for him. How do you explain to a child that the sibling he was so eager to meet was already gone? All I could do was cry, and all I could whisper to God was, *"Why? Why again?"*

The grief that followed was suffocating. Everywhere I looked, I saw reminders of what would never be. The nursery ideas I had been sketching out. The names I had been turning over in my heart. The prayers I had whispered over my womb. They all felt shattered, scattered like broken glass I didn't know how to gather up.

Carrying her, our Angelina Christine, for 20 weeks made the loss even harder. My body had nurtured her, protected her, and now I had to let her go. I grieved not only the baby I had lost, but the future I thought I was finally stepping into. Every kick I had longed to feel. Every milestone I thought was ahead. All of it disappeared in a moment.

And yet, even in the midst of that crushing grief, God's presence was there. Not in a way that erased the pain, but in a way that held me steady when I thought I might drown in it.

In hindsight, I see what I couldn't see then: obedience to God's voice matters more than the desires of my heart. Rushing ahead of His timing can lead to heartbreak. And yet — even when I disobeyed — His mercy never left me. He held me through the loss, even as I wrestled with guilt and grief.

This part of my journey reminds me that God's "no" is never to withhold good, but to protect. I didn't understand it at the time, but His ways are higher than mine. And even in the ashes of loss, His presence never left me.

STEPS TOWARD HOPE

Losing Angelina taught me something that I want to share with you: when God asks us to wait, it isn't because He wants to punish us — it's because His timing is protection. Waiting doesn't mean He's silent, and it doesn't mean He's forgotten.

If you find yourself in a season where you're tempted to rush ahead, pause instead. Be honest with God about your longing. Tell Him exactly how hard the waiting feels. Then, give Him room to respond before you move forward. Sometimes His direction comes through Scripture. Sometimes it comes as a whisper in your spirit. And sometimes it comes through the peace that stays when you lay something down. You don't have to force peace. It comes slowly, in the daily choice to lay your timeline down and whisper, *"Lord, I trust You, even here."*

You don't have to pretend the waiting is easy. But you also don't have to face it alone. If I could go back, I would tell myself to hold tighter to His voice than to my own timeline. That's how fragile hope becomes lasting hope — not by forcing the outcome, but by trusting the One who sees the whole story.

Reflection Questions:

1. Have you ever moved forward with something before seeking God's direction?
2. How did that decision impact your relationship with Him?
3. What does trusting God's timing look like in your current season?

Journaling Prompt: Write about a time you heard God speak clearly — even if you didn't listen right away. What did He teach you through that experience?

Your Reflections
Use this space to write your thoughts, prayers, or reflections as God speaks to your heart.

_____

_____

_____

_____

_____

_____

_____

_____

_____

_____

_____

_____

10

A Mother's Praise

Scripture: *"I will bless the Lord at all times; his praise shall continually be in my mouth."* — Psalm 34:1 (ESV)

After experiencing yet another ectopic pregnancy several years later, I lost my left fallopian tube. The weight of that loss pressed hard on me, and the timing made it worse. My sister-in-law, Shawnta, had scheduled me to sing on the praise team for Mother's Day.

When I called her to protest, broken and exhausted, she gently but firmly said, *"You have a decision to make. You can give the enemy the victory that day and stay in bed, or you can get up there and praise God with your whole heart — not because of what you see, but because you know the victory is already yours."*

Praise was the last thing I thought I had left in me. My body ached. My spirit groaned. My prayers felt too tired to rise above a whisper. But praise? Praise didn't demand perfection. It didn't require answers. It simply required presence — mine, and God's. Shawnta's bold words shifted my focus. I chose to praise Him. I refused to allow my situation to rob me of that sacred exchange with my Lord.

Somehow, praise became my anchor in the storm. Not just in church, but at home too.

It didn't always look like the loud, energetic worship I had known in services. At first, it was quieter. It whispered through tears. It sang softly in the stillness of nights when I clutched a pillow in arms that longed to hold a baby. It clung to promises I had written down, reading them aloud when fear came to taunt me.

Praising God in the middle of pain didn't erase the pain — but it reframed it. It reminded me that suffering wasn't the end of the story. That even when everything around me shook, God was unshakable.

I praised Him when the test was negative.

I praised Him when the silence of waiting felt unbearable.

I praised Him not because I always felt like it, but because He was still worthy of it.

And every time I lifted my voice or heart to Him, something shifted. My circumstances didn't vanish, but my perspective did. Praise pulled my eyes away from what I lacked and fixed them on the One who lacks nothing.

Worship as Warfare

In the hardest parts of the journey, when prayers felt weak and answers delayed, I learned to fight differently: I learned to worship.

Worship wasn't just a response to victory — it became the weapon that carried me through the battle. When I sang through tears, when I lifted my hands with trembling faith, I was declaring to the enemy: *"You have not won."* Worship reminded my soul of who God is — not based on what He had done yet, but based on what He had already promised.

There were days I didn't have the strength for long prayers. But I could put on worship music. I could sing a simple truth like, *"You are good,"* until my heart caught up. In those moments, I wasn't denying my pain. I was positioning my spirit in hope.

Scripture says, *"Yet you are holy, enthroned on the praises of Israel"* (Psalm 22:3). That means when we worship, heaven invades our situation. And where God is, chains break. Healing flows. Peace settles. Joy returns.

If you're still waiting, still aching, still wrestling — don't wait until the breakthrough to worship. Let worship lead you to the breakthrough.

Worship is not passive. It is warfare. And your praise is powerful.

Steps Toward Hope

If worship feels impossible in your pain, you are not alone. I've been there. There were days when my body ached, my prayers felt empty, and the only thing I could muster was a tear slipping down my cheek. On those days, worship didn't look like raised hands or a loud song. It began with a trembling whisper: *"God, I need You."* That whisper was worship.

Sometimes all I could do was put on a worship song and let the words wash over me until they became my own. Other times I sat in stillness, my palms open in surrender because I didn't have the strength to lift them high. Even my silence — offered to Him — became worship.

There were moments when I couldn't find my own voice, but I could sit under the sound of others lifting theirs. In those times, their songs carried me until I had the courage to join again. And sometimes, I wrote my worship instead of singing it — scribbled prayers like, *"Even though I don't understand, I choose to trust You."*

What I've learned is that worship isn't about how loud, how polished, or how strong we feel. It's simply about turning our hearts toward God — in the smallest ways, in the quietest places — and declaring, "Even here, You are worthy." And every single time I made that choice, no matter how weak I felt, I found that heaven leaned in.

REFLECTION QUESTIONS:

1. What does it mean for you to praise God *before* the promise is fulfilled?
2. How has worship sustained you in a season of disappointment or grief?
3. In what ways can you begin using worship as a form of spiritual warfare in your current situation?
4. What breakthrough might God be preparing through your praise?

JOURNALING PROMPT

Write a personal worship declaration. Even if you're still in the waiting phase, speak life and truth over your situation. Begin with the phrase: **"God, even now I will praise You because..."** and let your spirit lead.

Your Reflections
Use this space to write your thoughts, prayers, or reflections as God speaks to your heart.

_____

_____

_____

_____

_____

_____

_____

_____

_____

_____

_____

_____

_____

11

A Vision of Hope

Scripture: *"In the last days, God says, I will pour out my Spirit on all people. Your sons and daughters will prophesy, your young men will see visions."* — Acts 2:17 (NIV)

By the spring of 2008, I had walked through years of disappointment and loss. Miscarriages. Failed treatments. Surgeries that left scars on both my body and my heart. Each experience chipped away at my hope, yet deep down, I still longed for God to write a miracle into my story.

That Easter Sunday, it felt like He had.

On a quiet morning before church, I decided — almost absentmindedly — to take a pregnancy test. I had taken so many before, always bracing myself for disappointment. But this time, the test was positive. I was pregnant — and it had happened naturally, without medication.

The weight of that moment still brings tears to my eyes. It wasn't just a pregnancy test. It was Easter Sunday — resurrection day, the day life triumphed over death. From the depths of my heart, I believed this was it. This was the breakthrough. This was the promise fulfilled. I wasted no time in telling EVERYONE!

But only a short time later, everything shifted. I wasn't bleeding, but I felt the pain — sharp, unmistakable, undeniable. In an instant, I knew. I didn't need anyone to explain. My heart sank as I realized I was facing it all over again: another ectopic pregnancy. Another surgery. Another goodbye.

The joy of Easter morning collided with the crushing weight of loss. The miracle I thought was here slipped through my fingers before I could even hold it. That knowledge hit like a tidal wave. This was one of the darkest valleys of my journey. And yet, even there, God was already at work.

When our church gathered to pray over me before surgery, something happened that would later change the trajectory of our story. As Consuelo prayed, God spoke directly to her heart: *"You are meant to help Lisa."*

At first, she resisted. *"Lord, I can't relate to her pain. I've never battled infertility."* But God's response was gentle and firm: *"Yes, I know. That's why I chose you."*

The weight of those words was too great to carry alone. Immediately after service, Consuelo went to Pastor Marty and shared what God had spoken. Together, they prayed, and then went to her husband, Jason. This wasn't a rash or emotional decision — it was brought into spiritual covering and confirmed within her marriage covenant. Jason listened, prayed, and agreed: this was indeed from the Lord.

That step of obedience planted a seed of hope in the natural — one that God Himself would later water with confirmation to me.

For months, Chris and I had prayed, fasted, and gone back and forth about what direction we should take. We debated every possibility, weighed every option, and still felt like we were standing in the dark. Nothing seemed clear. Every door we considered brought new questions, and my heart grew more weary with each passing week.

Then, one Sunday morning, something in me broke. Before church, I went to God in prayer with a desperation I couldn't hold back anymore. Through tears I told Him, "Lord, I can't figure this out. I don't know what to do next. We have prayed and fasted, we've tried to reason it out, but I need You. I need Your direction, and I need it to be so clear that I won't be able to doubt it's You." It wasn't eloquent. It wasn't planned. It was the raw cry of a daughter who needed her Father's voice.

Later that morning, I stood on the stage with the praise team, lifting my voice in worship. I wasn't thinking about infertility. I wasn't even asking for a vision. I was simply doing what I was created to do — honoring God in song and leading His people into His presence. But in that moment of surrender, when my heart had finally let go of striving, He answered.

And then, in a sudden flash of divine clarity, I saw her — Consuelo — standing there, visibly pregnant, carrying my child.

The image was vivid, filled with peace that stilled my soul. It wasn't wishful thinking. It wasn't imagination. It was a holy moment. God was confirming to me what He had already spoken to her: this was the path He had chosen for us.

Looking back, I see how significant it was that the vision came in the middle of worship. Worship had always been my weapon — the way I fought when I had no strength left. It was in worship that I had previously experienced breakthrough, and once again, God chose that atmosphere to release His direction. Worship cleared the fog of fear just long enough for me to see His plan with clarity.

That's the power of worship as warfare: it shifts the atmosphere, silences the enemy, and opens space for God's voice. I wasn't striving. I wasn't begging. I was just worshiping — and in that posture, God handed me a vision of hope.

From that moment forward, I knew we were stepping into a new chapter. The losses were real, but so was the promise. And for the first time in a long time, I allowed myself to believe again: God's plan was not finished with me.

Steps Toward Hope

Looking back, I realize the vision God gave me didn't come because I had prayed all the right prayers or done all the right things. It came when I finally let go of trying to figure everything out on my own. After months of fasting, praying, and debating every option, I reached the end of myself and whispered, "God, I can't do this anymore. I need You to make it clear." That surrender became the doorway for Him to speak.

If you're in a season of waiting, I want you to know this: God is not hiding from you. He longs to meet you in your honesty. Your prayers don't have to be polished or perfect — sometimes the most powerful ones are the ones that come through tears. And even when you don't hear a vision or an audible word, He has a thousand ways to let you know He's near.

For me, worship became the place where His voice broke through. When I lifted my eyes off the questions and back onto Him, the fog lifted just enough for me to see His plan. You may not get the same kind of moment, but you can trust that He will speak to you in the way you need most. His voice always carries peace, even when His direction stretches your faith.

So if you are desperate for clarity, don't be afraid to stop striving. Pour out your heart to Him, then make room for Him to answer. It might come in worship, in Scripture, or in the wise counsel of someone you trust. However He chooses, you can be sure of this: He will not leave you without direction.

Reflection Questions:

1. Have you ever received a vision, dream, or word from God?
2. How do you discern when something is from God versus your own desires?
3. What would it look like to trust a promise before you see it fulfilled?

Journaling Prompt: Write about a moment when God spoke clearly to your heart. How did it shape your faith or decisions afterward?

Your Reflections
Use this space to write your thoughts, prayers, or reflections as God speaks to your heart.

12

The Impossible Path

Scripture: *"Jesus replied, 'What is impossible with man is possible with God.'"* — Luke 18:27 (NIV)

There was nothing conventional or easy about the journey we were about to embark on. The idea of using a gestational carrier was overwhelming. It was expensive. It was complicated. And frankly, it felt impossible. But when God gives you a word, He also gives you the grace to walk it out.

Chris and I began praying, fasting, and seeking counsel. We didn't know where to start. We didn't know how the pieces could ever come together. But what we didn't realize at the time was that God had already gone before us.

Years earlier, my parents had sold us their house with a gift of equity. At the time, none of us understood the significance of that blessing. But God did. When the moment came, that very equity became the resource that paid for the process to bring our children into the world. Provision had been planted years before we even knew there would be a need.

And the miracles didn't stop there. The fertility clinic we needed had a six-month waiting list — sometimes longer. But when we called, they had just received a cancellation. What should have been months of waiting turned into an appointment within a week.

Step after step, we saw God's hand. Paperwork that should have been delayed was expedited. Approvals that should have taken weeks came through in days. People went out of their way to help us. Doors that should have been locked swung wide open. Every time we hit what looked like a wall, God created a way straight through it. It was as if He was saying, *"You're finally walking in step with Me. Now watch what I will do."*

For years, I had carried silent questions about my 20-week miscarriage. The doctors could never give me a definitive answer for why it happened. That lack of clarity only fueled my self-defeat. The enemy used it to whisper lies: *This was your fault. Your body failed. You weren't meant to carry life.* I believed those lies more often than I admitted.

But at our very first appointment with the fertility specialist, God brought truth to light. After reviewing my medical records, he sat with us and explained that I had experienced a **protein S deficiency** during that pregnancy — a condition that can lead to blood clotting issues and pregnancy loss. Suddenly, what had been a question mark for years was finally answered.

I can't describe the relief that came in that moment. It didn't erase the grief, but it lifted the crushing weight of blame I had carried. I realized the loss wasn't because of something I had done wrong, and it wasn't because I was "broken." It was a medical condition. And knowing the truth helped silence the lies I had lived under for so long.

Even in that, I saw God's mercy: He was not only making a way forward for us, He was also healing places of shame from the past.

Was it easy? Not at all. There were still moments of fear, questions that lingered, and emotions that threatened to overwhelm. But through it all, the journey was marked by peace.

Not the peace that comes from perfect circumstances, but the peace that comes from knowing God Himself was walking beside us through every unknown. The kind of peace Jesus promised in John 14:27: *"Peace I leave with you; my peace I give you. I do not give to you as the world gives. Do not let your hearts be troubled and do not be afraid."*

This was the impossible path. And yet, with God, it was becoming possible.

Steps Toward Hope

Walking the "impossible path" can feel overwhelming — too costly, too complicated, too far beyond what you can manage. I know that feeling well. But this chapter of my journey taught me something life-changing: God always goes before us. The provision, the people, the opportunities — so often they are already in place before we even know we'll need them.

If you are standing in front of what feels impossible, start here: bring your fears honestly before God. Tell Him what feels too big, too heavy, or too unknown. He isn't intimidated by your questions. In fact, He delights in carrying the weight you were never meant to shoulder alone.

Then, take one step. It doesn't have to be the whole journey at once. For us, it was making a phone call, showing up for an appointment, or filling out one form at a time. Every small step became an invitation for God to move in ways we couldn't.

And finally, hold on to truth when lies try to creep in. For years, I carried guilt over my miscarriage until a doctor gave me clarity. Maybe you're carrying blame too. Hear this: your loss is not your fault. Your worth is not determined by what your body could or couldn't do. Let God's truth replace the enemy's lies.

The impossible path may not get easier overnight. But with each step of surrender, you'll see God's fingerprints — proof that He's been making a way for you all along.

Reflection Questions:

1. Have you ever walked a path that felt too big, too expensive, or too unknown?
2. How did God meet you in your step of obedience?
3. What would it look like to trust God's provision for the path ahead of you?

Journaling Prompt: Write about a time when you were afraid to obey God because of what it might cost. What did He show you through that experience?

Your Reflections

Use this space to write your thoughts, prayers, or reflections as God speaks to your heart.

_____

_____

_____

_____

_____

_____

_____

_____

_____

_____

_____

_____

_____

13

Twists and Turns

Scripture: *"Not only so, but we also glory in our sufferings, because we know that suffering produces perseverance."* — Romans 5:3 (NIV)

One of the first miracles we experienced in the gestational carrier journey was how perfectly our bodies aligned. Normally, women going through this process need medication to regulate their cycles and bring everything into sync. But God did what medicine could not. Without a single pill or injection, my body and Consuelo's lined up exactly the way they needed to. It was as if God Himself was setting the stage, arranging the timing, and reminding us that His hand was on every detail.

With that encouragement, we moved forward into our first embryo transfer, filled with hope. I remember walking into the clinic with so much confidence, almost giddy with anticipation — like we were finally standing on the edge of our miracle.

And at first, it worked. The doctors confirmed that the transfer had taken — Consuelo was pregnant. For the first time, we carried the joy of knowing that life was growing, that our child was finally on the way.

But only a few weeks later, that hope unraveled. The pregnancy didn't last. Another loss. Another goodbye.

This one cut differently. It wasn't only my grief this time. It was Consuelo's too. She had given so much of herself — her prayers, her body, her willingness to stand in the gap for us. She had walked into this with full faith and expectation, and now she, too, had to sit with the ache of another "no." We carried the sorrow together, and though it was heavy, I thank God we didn't have to carry it alone.

Still, the questions came rushing in. *Had we misunderstood the vision? Was this a sign we weren't meant to take this path? Had we missed God somewhere along the way?* I replayed every detail, desperately searching for answers. The enemy wanted me to spiral — to conclude that God had abandoned us.

But in the middle of that heartbreak, when doubt was loudest, the Holy Spirit whispered: *"I didn't bring you this far to abandon you now."*

That whisper became my anchor in the storm. It reminded me that one loss didn't cancel the promise. One setback didn't erase God's faithfulness.

And Jason — Consuelo's husband — became a steady voice of faith when ours felt weak. No matter what the circumstances looked like, he refused to waver. He reminded all of us: *"God said, and that settles it. We have to have faith and confidence in that."* Jason's conviction gave us courage. When the weight of disappointment threatened to drown us, his voice reminded us to stand firm in what God had already spoken.

So we chose to try again. Not out of recklessness or blind desperation, but out of renewed faith. We reminded ourselves daily that God never promised the journey would be easy — only that He would be faithful to finish what He started.

We prepared for the second transfer with hearts surrendered. We prayed. We fasted. We surrounded the process with worship, because by then we had learned: worship is our greatest weapon in the waiting.

And this time — there were two heartbeats.

Steps Toward Hope

Disappointment after hope can feel even heavier than the first loss. I know what it's like to think, *Maybe I heard God wrong. Maybe I shouldn't have believed so boldly.* But what I learned in that season is this: one setback does not erase God's promise. His faithfulness doesn't waver, even when outcomes don't look the way we prayed they would.

If you're facing a twist in your story, I want to encourage you to pause and breathe before you draw conclusions. Don't let the enemy convince you that one "no" means God has abandoned you. Sometimes the greatest act of faith is simply to keep showing up — to keep praying, to keep worshiping, to keep moving forward when every part of you wants to quit.

It also helps to borrow faith when yours feels weak. In our story, Jason's unshakable conviction that *"God said, and that settles it"* carried us through days when doubt tried to drown us. Surround yourself with voices that call you back to what God has spoken. If you don't have those voices yet, pray for them. God will send people who can remind you of His truth when your own heart is weary.

And finally, give yourself permission to hope again. Hope can feel risky after loss — but it's also how we persevere. Try again, not because you're strong enough to handle another disappointment, but because God is strong enough to carry you through whatever comes. He hasn't brought you this far to leave you now.

Reflection Questions:

1. How do you respond when something you were sure about doesn't work out?
2. What helps you persevere when your faith is tested?
3. Have you ever had to try again, even when you were afraid to hope?

Journaling Prompt: Reflect on a time you had to trust God after a setback. What fears did you face? What did God teach you about perseverance?

Your Reflections
Use this space to write your thoughts, prayers, or reflections as God speaks to your heart.

_____

_____

_____

_____

_____

_____

_____

_____

_____

_____

_____

_____

_____

14

A Double Portion

SCRIPTURE: *"INSTEAD OF YOUR SHAME YOU WILL RECEIVE A DOUBLE PORTION..."* — ISAIAH 61:7 (NIV)

When we found out we were having twins, I couldn't stop crying. It wasn't just joy — it was the overwhelming awareness of God's kindness.

What made it even more incredible was that this transfer had been done with frozen embryos, which the doctors explained carried lower odds of success compared to fresh transfers. They told us the chances of even one healthy baby were only about 56%, and the odds of twins were just 14.9%. And yet, God did what statistics said was unlikely. After years of loss and waiting, He had given us not one child, but two.

It felt like a divine declaration: *I see you. I didn't forget.*

Jason, who had stood so firmly in faith through every twist and turn, rejoiced with us as if he had known all along — because in his heart, he had. His constant reminders, *"God said and we have to have confidence in that,"* now rang like prophecy fulfilled. God had not only answered our prayers but exceeded them with abundance.

We named them early — Matthias and Israel. Their names weren't chosen lightly; they were declarations. Matthias means "gift of God," and he truly was. Israel means "prince who prevails with God." Together, their names told the story of our journey: God gives good gifts, and He causes His children to prevail. These boys were not only answers to our prayers but living testaments of God's covenant promises.

Even before they were born, we spoke life over them. We prayed specific prayers for their health, their callings, their character. We asked God to mold us into the kind of parents they would need. Naming them wasn't just identity — it was prophecy. It was planting seeds of destiny.

And as I looked ahead to becoming a mother of twins, something else stirred in my heart — something I hadn't expected. For years, I had loved Christopher as if he were my own. From the time he was three years old, I poured myself into raising him, guiding him, and trying to be the mother he needed me to be. But when I held Matthias and Israel for the first time, I realized there had been a part of me holding back without even knowing it. Not because I didn't love Christopher — I did — but because I didn't yet understand the depth of a mother's love. Their birth unlocked something inside me. Suddenly, I could see how I had cheated Christopher of the fullness of that love, not by choice, but by limitation. And in His kindness, God used the twins to expand my capacity, to show me how to love Christopher even more completely. That, too, was part of the double portion. God hadn't only given me two more sons; He had healed and deepened my love for the son He had entrusted me with years earlier.

In those months, I began to understand something profound: God doesn't just give you children — He entrusts you with the ones you are meant to parent. It wasn't about replacing what I had lost or filling an ache with "any" child. It was about stewarding the exact lives He had ordained to come through us, in His timing, in His way. Trusting that truth brought me a peace I had never known before.

That pregnancy wasn't without challenges, but we were surrounded by prayer. We had a community of believers standing in the gap, reminding us of God's promises when fear tried to creep back in. Their faith became a covering.

For the first time in a long time, I allowed myself to prepare — to truly believe the miracle was happening. I bought baby clothes. I filled journals with prayers and dreams for their future. I let myself imagine what it would feel like to hold them. And with every ultrasound update, every milestone, every tiny heartbeat echoing through the speakers, God whispered the same reminder: *I am faithful.*

Steps Toward Hope

When I look back on this season, I see that God's blessings often carry layers I could never have anticipated. I thought the miracle was simply in having children after so many years of loss. But His double portion was bigger than that. Through Matthias and Israel, God not only answered the deepest cry of my heart but also expanded my ability to love Christopher in a fuller, richer way. I realized that abundance doesn't just come in numbers — it comes in the way God stretches us to love more deeply, forgive more freely, and live more fully.

If you are waiting for your own double portion, I encourage you not to overlook the quieter miracles happening along the way. God's abundance may begin with a shift inside of you before it ever shows up around you. For me, it started with the healing of old wounds and the softening of places I didn't even know needed His touch. That healing allowed me to step into motherhood with an open heart, no longer loving with limitation, but with the fullness of grace God had poured into me.

Hope grows when we begin to trust that God's promises are not bound by statistics, timelines, or circumstances. Doctors gave us odds that made our outcome seem unlikely, but God reminded me that His Word holds greater weight than numbers on a chart. He showed me that His abundance can break through in ways we least expect — through restored relationships, renewed vision, or even a deeper awareness of His presence while we wait.

If your miracle hasn't come yet, don't dismiss the small ways God may already be preparing your heart. Sometimes the double portion is not just about what He places in your arms, but about what He cultivates within your spirit along the way. And when the fulfillment of His promise does come, you will discover that He has not only given you what you asked for, but also grown you into someone who can carry it with joy, strength, and gratitude.

Reflection Questions:

1. Have you ever experienced a blessing that exceeded your expectations? What did it teach you about God's nature?
2. Can you look back and see a time when God expanded your capacity to love — perhaps in parenting, marriage, friendship, or even in how you see yourself?
3. In what ways has God entrusted you with people to nurture or influence, even if they didn't come into your life in the way you first expected?
4. How do you respond when long-awaited prayers are finally answered — with gratitude, with hesitation, or with a deeper faith?

Journaling Prompt: Write about a moment when God surprised you with abundance. How did it shift your view of Him and His promises?

Your Reflections
Use this space to write your thoughts, prayers, or reflections as
God speaks to your heart.

15

Behind the Promise

There are moments in life when you know you're standing on holy ground — not because of where you are, but because of what God is doing. Walking through the gestational carrier journey with Jason and Consuelo Murrell was one of those moments.

From the very beginning, it was clear this was no ordinary arrangement. It was a divine assignment. Their willingness to carry not just a pregnancy, but our promise, left me in awe of what selfless obedience to God can look like.

I remember the first ultrasound we attended together. Seeing the flicker of life on that screen — not within me, but within her — was surreal. It was humbling. It was sacred. I cried, not only because I saw my children, but because I witnessed the faith of a woman who said "yes" when God asked something extraordinary of her.

There were moments of fear — would the pregnancy hold? Would complications arise? Would my heart survive the waiting again? But Consuelo's faith was steady. Jason's voice of faith was unwavering. Time and again, he reminded us all: *"God said, and we have to have confidence in that."* Together, they carried the promise not just in body, but in spirit. They prayed over our babies, sang to them, and loved them as fiercely as we did.

The day our boys were born was a day I will never forget. I watched life come into the world through the sacrifice and strength of someone who chose to make our burden her calling. As I held our sons for the first time, the weight of years of loss melted into one overwhelming truth: God is faithful.

This chapter of the journey was not what I pictured when I first dreamed of motherhood. But it was more miraculous than I could have imagined. It took a village — and in the center of that village stood Jason and Consuelo, whose obedience and faith helped deliver our long-awaited joy.

Their names are written in our story forever.

REFLECTION: STANDING WITH OTHERS IN THEIR PROMISE

Not every calling looks the same. Sometimes God asks us to carry a promise of our own. Other times, He asks us to help carry someone else's. Jason and Consuelo reminded me that obedience is rarely convenient, but it is always powerful. Their willingness to say "yes" became the very bridge God used to bring life into our family.

You may not be called to carry a child for someone else, but you may be called to carry a burden in prayer, to speak words of faith when others are too weary, or to walk beside someone whose hope feels fragile. Scripture calls this *"bearing one another's burdens"* (Galatians 6:2), and it is one of the most Christlike ways we can love each other.

Who in your life needs you to stand firm in faith on their behalf? Who needs your prayers, your encouragement, or simply your presence? Don't underestimate the power of your "yes" — it could be the very thing God uses to help deliver someone else's miracle.

Steps Toward Hope

Walking with Jason and Consuelo through this journey taught me something I'll carry for the rest of my life: God rarely intends for us to walk through seasons of waiting, pain, or even promise alone. Sometimes He sends people to stand with us, and sometimes He calls us to be those people for others. Both are holy assignments.

There were days when my faith was threadbare, when disappointment pressed so heavily that I could barely find words to pray. In those moments, Jason and Consuelo stood in the gap. Their prayers covered me when mine faltered. Their faith steadied me when mine wavered. Their "yes" to God's call gave me strength to keep saying "yes" to Him, too.

If you find yourself waiting on a promise, ask God to show you the people He's placed around you to help carry the weight. Sometimes His provision looks like community — the friend who checks in, the pastor who prays, the family member who quietly believes with you. Let their faith remind you of what is true when your own feels weak.

And if you are in a season where God is asking you to stand with someone else, lean into it with obedience and joy. You may not see the full picture of what your presence or encouragement will accomplish, but your willingness could become the very bridge someone else needs to keep believing.

Hope multiplies in community. When we carry one another's burdens, we share in the miracle God is writing. And in the process, we come to see His faithfulness not only in our own stories but also in the lives of those we've had the honor to stand beside.

Reflection Questions:

1. Have you ever been strengthened by someone else's faith when yours felt weak?
2. How might God be asking you to stand with someone in their season of waiting?
3. What "yes" could you give today that might open the door for someone else's breakthrough?

Journaling Prompt:

Write about a time someone's faith carried you. Then, ask God to show you who He may be asking you to carry in prayer, encouragement, or action. What practical step can you take this week to stand in faith with them?

Your Reflections
Use this space to write your thoughts, prayers, or reflections as
God speaks to your heart.

_____

_____

_____

_____

_____

_____

_____

_____

_____

_____

_____

_____

_____

16

Labor of Love

SCRIPTURE: *"CHILDREN ARE A HERITAGE FROM THE LORD, OFFSPRING A REWARD FROM HIM."* — PSALM 127:3 (NIV)

The day finally arrived. I stood in the hospital room, watching the miracle unfold right in front of me. Consuelo, who had carried our sons with such strength and grace, was in labor. Every contraction, every breath, every moment felt sacred. She had given of herself in a way I will never be able to repay, and I silently thanked God for her obedience and selflessness.

It's hard to put into words the emotions of that day. Gratitude, awe, nervous anticipation — they all rushed over me in waves. My heart raced as I realized: *This is it.* The moment I had prayed for, fought for, wept for. The moment my arms would finally no longer be empty.

When the time came, we were allowed in the operating room for the delivery. Consuelo amazed me. She delivered our sons completely naturally — no medication, no shortcuts. She stayed strong and steady through every contraction, never losing focus. And Jason was right there at her side, a rock in the storm, keeping her encouraged and centered. They were a team, working in perfect rhythm, carrying the weight of this miracle together with grace and determination. Watching them gave me a new respect for what sacrificial love really looks like.

The room itself was filled with bright lights, medical staff, and the sound of steady instructions — but more than that, it was filled with love, faith, and the unmistakable presence of God. And then, it happened. My sons entered the world.

I wept as I held each of them for the first time. Tears streamed down my face, not only for the miracle of their lives but for the years of waiting, loss, and surrender that had led to this moment. I pressed them against me, inhaling their newborn scent, feeling their tiny weight in my arms. For so long, I had feared this day might never come. But here they were — flesh of my flesh, miracles in my embrace.

So many emotions swirled through me — awe, relief, disbelief, joy — but above all, gratitude. Gratitude to a God who had carried me through valleys that once threatened to destroy me. Gratitude that He had not just answered my prayers but had done so abundantly, giving me not one child, but two. Gratitude that He had entrusted Matthias and Israel to me — handpicked sons with a destiny only He could write.

As I held them close, flashes of my journey came rushing back: the sterile hospital rooms where I wept after loss, the quiet nights when I begged God for an answer, the moments I nearly gave up hope. Every prayer, every tear, every heartbreak had led here. And suddenly, I could see it all clearly — *nothing had been wasted.* Every valley had only made this mountaintop more breathtaking.

Matthias and Israel were here — healthy, strong, and full of promise. Their names were not just names but declarations:

Matthias, *"gift of God,"* and Israel, *"prince who prevails with God."* They were living testimonies of His faithfulness.

As I looked into their tiny faces, I felt the weight of God's redemption settle on my heart like a warm blanket. He had truly turned my mourning into dancing. He had taken my ashes and given me beauty. He had filled my empty arms — but even more than that, He had restored my hope.

Steps Toward Hope

The day Matthias and Israel were born will forever remind me that God's promises, no matter how delayed, are never denied when He has spoken them. But holding them in my arms also taught me something deeper: answered prayers don't erase the journey, they redeem it.

For so long, I imagined that once I had children in my arms, the ache of loss would vanish. But the truth is, healing didn't come from a single moment — it came from seeing how God had been faithful all along. Every detour, every heartbreak, every "not yet" was part of Him shaping my story so that His glory could shine even brighter in the fulfillment.

If you're still waiting, I want you to know this: your miracle may not look exactly like mine, but God is faithful to complete what He has begun in you. Don't despise the waiting — let it deepen your faith. Don't believe the lie that God has forgotten you — hold on to the truth that He is weaving something beyond what you can see.

And when your promise does come — whether in the way you imagined or in a way you never expected — pause to recognize His hand in it. Celebrate it. Mark it down. Write it in your journal. Tell your story. Because your testimony will become someone else's hope.

God never wastes a single tear. Every prayer you've prayed is collected, and one day, in His perfect timing, you will see the redemption of your waiting.

Reflection Questions:

1. What does it feel like to witness God's promise fulfilled?
2. How do you celebrate moments of answered prayer?
3. Who in your life has helped carry you to your miracle?

Journaling Prompt: Write a letter to God expressing your gratitude for the answered prayers in your life — even the ones that came differently than you expected.

Your Reflections
Use this space to write your thoughts, prayers, or reflections as
God speaks to your heart.

17

Naming the Promise

Scripture: *"You shall be called by a new name that the mouth of the Lord will bestow."* — Isaiah 62:2 (ESV)

Naming our sons was one of the most significant spiritual acts of our journey. We didn't just want names that sounded nice — we wanted names that declared destiny. Names that would remind us of what God had done and what we believed He would do in their lives.

Matthias means *"gift of God,"* and every time we say his name, we remember the years of waiting and the miracle of God's provision. **Israel** means *"prince who prevails with God."* His name reminds us that through every battle, every struggle, God is not distant — He contends for us, and with Him, we will prevail.

But what God showed me is that this wasn't just about my children. This was about a principle in His kingdom: *names carry power.*

Throughout Scripture, we see God rename people to declare their new identity in Him. Abram became Abraham, the father of many nations. Jacob, the deceiver, became Israel, the one who prevails with God. Simon became Peter, the rock on which the church would be built. Every name carried destiny. Every word spoken carried weight.

That's why we chose our sons' names intentionally. We wanted them rooted in Scripture, in truth, in the character of God Himself. We knew that when we spoke their names, we weren't just calling them to dinner or waking them up for school — we were declaring their God-given identity.

And the same is true for us. As parents, we have the privilege of shaping the spiritual atmosphere our children grow in. But even beyond parenting, each of us holds the responsibility of what we speak over ourselves and others. Proverbs 18:21 reminds us that "the tongue has the power of life and death." With every word, we are either planting life or death, hope or despair, blessing or curse.

That's why I will never take lightly the calling of speaking life — over my sons, over my family, and over myself. Because words shape worlds. Names call out destinies. And declarations of faith can shift the course of a life.

So as you read this, I want to ask: *What names are you answering to?* Are they the ones the enemy whispered in your darkest moments — unworthy, barren, broken? Or are they the names God has spoken over you — chosen, beloved, redeemed?

Friend, you are not what has been done to you. You are not what you've lost. You are who God says you are. And just as He gave me the privilege of naming my children as declarations of His promise, He has named you as His own.

Steps Toward Hope

When we named Matthias and Israel, it was more than a parent's choice — it was a declaration of God's faithfulness and their destiny. That experience opened my eyes to how powerful names and words really are.

For years, I had answered to names the enemy whispered over me: *broken, barren, forgotten.* Those names shaped how I saw myself, how I prayed, and even how I walked into rooms. But God never called me those things. He called me *daughter, chosen, beloved, redeemed.* And learning to answer to His voice instead of the enemy's changed everything.

Maybe you've been living under false names, too. Perhaps pain, loss, or even the careless words of others have tried to define you. If that's the case, I encourage you to pause and ask God: *What name do You call me?* Then hold tightly to what He speaks. Write it down. Speak it out loud. Let it become louder than the lies.

And if you are a parent — whether to biological children, stepchildren, adopted children, or spiritual sons and daughters — don't underestimate the power of what you call them. Every word you speak over them is like seed being planted in their hearts. Speak life. Call out destiny. Remind them who God says they are, even on the days they forget.

This isn't about perfect words or dramatic declarations. It's about aligning your voice with His truth. Because when you begin to call yourself, your children, and those around you by the names God has spoken, hope takes root — and destiny unfolds.

Reflection Questions:

1. What names or labels have others spoken over you that you've struggled to let go of?
2. How do you think those words have shaped the way you see yourself or your circumstances?
3. What new name or truth from God's Word do you sense Him speaking over you today?
4. In what ways can you begin speaking life over your children, family, or even yourself?

Journaling Prompt: If you could rename a difficult season in your life with a word of redemption, what would it be? Write about the new meaning that season holds.

Your Reflections
Use this space to write your thoughts, prayers, or reflections as God speaks to your heart.

_____

_____

_____

_____

_____

_____

_____

_____

_____

_____

_____

_____

_____

18

For the One Who Still Waits

Scripture: *"But those who hope in the Lord will renew their strength. They will soar on wings like eagles; they will run and not grow weary, they will walk and not be faint."* — Isaiah 40:31 (NIV)

Dear friend,

If you're still waiting, still aching, still wondering when your promise will come — this chapter is for you.

I may not know the details of your journey. I don't know how many tears you've cried, how many prayers you've whispered, or how many times you've fought to believe when everything around you said it was over. But I do know this: you are perfectly and wonderfully made by God (Psalm 139:14). Nothing that has happened to you — no diagnosis, no loss, no mistake — can cancel His promises over your life.

You are His daughter. Chosen. Seen. Loved (Ephesians 1:4, Isaiah 43:1).

God cares about the desires of your heart because He is the One who placed them there (Psalm 37:4). The longing you feel is not a flaw. It is evidence that you were created for love, for fruitfulness, for purpose. He is not punishing you, and He is not withholding good from you (Psalm 84:11). Even in the silence, even in the stillness, He is working. If your miracle hasn't come yet, that doesn't mean it never will. If your path looks different from others', that doesn't make it any less divine. God's timing is not a delay — it is a masterpiece unfolding. And when His hand is weaving the threads of your life, nothing is wasted.

I pray that my story has reminded you that you are not alone. That hope is still possible. That miracles still happen — often in the ways we least expect.

So keep holding on. Keep praying. Keep trusting. When your strength runs out, lean into His. When your faith feels fragile, let Him be your anchor. His arms are strong enough for both your grief and your hope.

You are not forgotten. You are not forsaken. You are still **Hope Full.**

Steps Toward Hope

Waiting is one of the hardest places to live. It stretches you, tests you, and sometimes feels like it's breaking you. I know because I've sat in that same space — wondering if God saw me, if He had forgotten me, if I would always live in the ache of "not yet."

But waiting is not wasted. In my own journey, I discovered that waiting is where roots grow deep. It's where trust is forged, not in outcomes, but in the character of God Himself. And it's where hope, even when fragile, becomes unshakable.

If you are still waiting, I want to encourage you to take small but steady steps that keep your heart tender toward God:

Begin by bringing Him your raw honesty. Don't dress up your prayers. Tell Him when you're angry, when you're tired, when you don't understand. He isn't offended by your pain — He longs to meet you there.

Surround yourself with voices that will remind you of truth when you forget. This might be friends who will pray with you, a church family that carries you in faith, or simply worship music filling your home when words feel hard to find.

And most of all, keep watch for glimpses of God's faithfulness — even in small things. A Scripture that speaks directly to your heart. A friend who shows up at just the right moment. A peace that comes in the middle of a storm. These are not coincidences; they are reminders that God is still moving, even in the waiting.

Friend, the waiting doesn't mean your story is over. It means God is still writing. And while you may not yet see the whole picture, you can trust that His pen never slips, and His heart toward you never wavers.

Reflection Questions:

1. What are you still waiting on God to do in your life?
2. How has the waiting shaped your faith — for better or for worse?
3. What promises are you holding onto, even when you can't yet see the outcome?

Journaling Prompt: Write a letter to your future self — the one who has seen God come through. What would you want her to remember about this season of waiting?

Your Reflections
Use this space to write your thoughts, prayers, or reflections as
God speaks to your heart.

Final Prayer

Almighty God, Miracle Worker, Faithful Father —

You alone are worthy of our praise. You are the God who brings life from barren places, who speaks hope into despair, and who redeems every broken story for Your glory. There is no wound too deep for Your healing, no wait too long for Your promise, no battle too hard for Your victory.

Lord, I boldly lift up every reader who has walked through these pages — women and men carrying heartbreak, disappointment, unanswered prayers, and deferred dreams. In the mighty name of Jesus, I declare that **their story is not over.** That **Your plans for them are still good.** That **miracles are still in motion even when they cannot yet be seen.**

I speak LIFE over every womb — physical and spiritual. I speak PEACE over every anxious heart. I speak RESTORATION over every broken place. Where there has been mourning, let there now be dancing. Where there has been fear, let faith rise up like a roaring flood.

You are not a God of delays — You are a God of perfect timing. Remind them, Holy Spirit, that You are closer than their next breath. May they trust You not just for the promise, but in the process.

Let testimonies be born from this book. Let chains fall. Let dead dreams resurrect. Let Your name be lifted high as proof that You still do the impossible.

I thank You for the miracle of my sons — and I pray boldly for the miracles still coming to those reading these words. May this book be more than a story — may it be a spark for breakthrough.

In the all-powerful, matchless name of Jesus Christ,

Amen and amen.

Acknowledgments

Writing this book has been one of the most sacred, vulnerable, and redemptive journeys of my life. I could not have done it alone — and I wouldn't have wanted to.

To my husband, Chris — your love, strength, and unwavering faith carried me through the hardest chapters of my story. You believed in me when I couldn't believe in myself. Thank you for walking this road with me, step by step.

To my sons — Christopher, Matthias, and Israel — you are living proof that God is faithful. Your laughter, your love, and your very lives are a miracle. You are my answered prayers.

To Jason and Consuelo Murrell — there are no words that can capture the magnitude of what you've given. Your obedience to God and your selfless love changed our lives forever. Thank you for being the vessel of God's promise.

To my mom — your steady love and constant encouragement have been an anchor in my life. You have prayed me through seasons of heartbreak and rejoiced with me in seasons of joy. Thank you for always being there.

To my dad — even though you passed after the twins were born, I know you were proud. I carry your strength and your faith with me. I wish you could see them grow, but I know you're watching from Heaven.

To Terry and Shawnta — thank you for always being willing to say the hard things in love. When we were tempted to give up, your truth and wisdom helped us stay the course.

To Pastor Marty Squires — thank you for standing in the gap with us, for your immovable faith, and for the words of encouragement you poured into us through every step of our journey. You celebrated with us in the victories and carried us with prayer in the waiting.

To Felix and Stacy Bonet — your words of strength and encouragement came exactly when we needed them most. In a season when our faith was tested, you helped give us the boost to keep believing.

To our church family — thank you for your prayers, your encouragement, and your spiritual covering. You stood in the gap, and your faith helped fuel ours.

To every friend, mentor, and prayer warrior who listened, cried, believed, and reminded me of who I am in Christ — thank you. You helped keep my hope alive.

And finally, **to the reader** — thank you for holding my story with tenderness and trust. I pray it becomes a part of your healing.

To God be all the glory. He writes the best stories.

Devotional Appendix

Here are seven short devotionals — one for each day of the week — drawn from the themes of this book. Use them to reflect, reset, and remember who God is in your waiting, your healing, and your hope.

Day 1: God Sees You
"You are the God who sees me." — Genesis 16:13 (NIV)

God saw Hagar in the wilderness — abandoned, mistreated, and alone. He sees you, too. Not just your smile, but your struggle. Not just your faith, but your fatigue. Rest today knowing that you are never invisible to Him.

Reflection: Where do you need to be reminded that God sees you?

Day 2: Hope in the Waiting
"The Lord is good to those who wait for him, to the soul who seeks him." — Lamentations 3:25 (ESV)

Waiting is not wasted when it is surrendered to God. He is shaping your heart, building your faith, and preparing your miracle.

Reflection: What has God grown in you during your waiting season?

Day 3: God Is Near to the Broken
"The Lord is close to the brokenhearted and saves those who are crushed in spirit." — Psalm 34:18 (NIV)

Grief does not disqualify you from God's presence — it draws Him closer. Bring Him your tears, and let Him be your refuge.

Reflection: What comfort has God provided in your sorrow?

Day 4: Peace That Doesn't Make Sense

"And the peace of God, which surpasses all understanding, will guard your hearts and your minds in Christ Jesus." — Philippians 4:7 (ESV)

Even in chaos, even in loss, God offers a peace that doesn't make sense to the world. It's not based on outcomes — it's based on His unchanging presence.

Reflection: Where do you need God's peace right now?

Day 5: He Fights for You

"The Lord will fight for you; you need only to be still." — Exodus 14:14 (NIV)

You do not fight your battles alone. God is not distant. He is actively defending, shielding, and making a way where there is none.

Reflection: What battle do you need to release into God's hands today?

Day 6: Beauty from Ashes

"He will give a crown of beauty for ashes, a joyous blessing instead of mourning." — Isaiah 61:3 (NLT)

God doesn't just remove pain — He redeems it. He transforms our deepest wounds into testimonies of His goodness. You are not your loss — you are His masterpiece in the making.

Reflection: What has God already begun to redeem in your story?

Day 7: God Finishes What He Starts

"Being confident of this, that he who began a good work in you will carry it on to completion." — Philippians 1:6 (NIV)

God is not done with you. The work He began — in your heart, your family, your future — He will finish. He is faithful to complete every promise.

Reflection: What promise do you need to hold onto with fresh faith today?

Declarations of Hope

When your faith feels shaky, speak the truth of God with boldness. These are not empty words — they are weapons of faith, rooted in the Word of God. Let them fill your mouth, renew your mind, and revive your spirit.

Speak them aloud. Declare them daily. Let them reshape your waiting into worship.

Declarations of Hope and Faith

1. **"God is not late. He is always right on time."** *(Habakkuk 2:3)*
2. **"My womb, my heart, and my life are not barren. They are being prepared for fruitfulness."** *(Exodus 23:26)*
3. **"I believe even when I do not see."** *(John 20:29)*
4. **"The same God who opened Sarah's womb is working miracles in my life."** *(Genesis 21:1-2)*
5. **"My tears are not wasted. They are being sown for joy."** *(Psalm 126:5)*
6. **"God is writing my story, and it will glorify Him."** *(Romans 8:28)*
7. **"Even in the waiting, I am growing stronger."** *(Isaiah 40:31)*
8. **"I will see the goodness of the Lord in the land of the living."** *(Psalm 27:13)*
9. **"God remembers me. He has not forgotten."** *(1 Samuel 1:19)*

10. **"I am Hope Full — because my hope is in Christ."**
(Hebrews 10:23)

Repeat them. Believe them. Live them.

You are not powerless — you are faith-filled. You are not forgotten — you are seen. You are not barren — you are blessed.

Let these truths guide your journey, strengthen your steps, and remind you: God is faithful.

Practical Prayer Strategy

How I Prayed Through the Waiting

Prayer during seasons of waiting doesn't have to be long, eloquent, or perfect. It just has to be real. Over time, I learned to build a rhythm of prayer that helped anchor my heart, renew my mind, and push back the lies of doubt. Here's what that looked like for me — and what might work for you.

1. BEGIN WITH WORSHIP

"Enter his gates with thanksgiving and his courts with praise..." — Psalm 100:4 Start by turning your focus to God's character, not your circumstances. Put on a worship song. Sing or speak words like: "You are faithful, You are near, You are my hope."

2. SPEAK THE WORD ALOUD

Choose 1–2 Scriptures and declare them out loud — even if your heart feels uncertain. Examples:

- "No good thing does He withhold..." (Psalm 84:11)
- "I will see the goodness of the Lord in the land of the living." (Psalm 27:13)

3. PRAY HONESTLY

Talk to God without filters. Tell Him how you feel. Cry if you need to. He can handle it. Example: "God, I don't understand, but I trust You. Help me trust You more."

4. ASK BOLDLY

Don't be afraid to ask specifically for what you need — healing, conception, peace, clarity. God honors persistent faith. (Luke 18:1–8)

5. LISTEN IN STILLNESS

Spend 2–5 minutes in quiet. Ask, "Lord, is there something You want to show me today?" Write down any Scripture, word, or thought that rises in your spirit.

6. KEEP A PRAYER JOURNAL

Write prayers, promises, and moments of encouragement you receive. On dark days, you'll need reminders of what God has already spoken.

7. END WITH A DECLARATION

Finish with a declaration of faith. Even if it's through tears, say something like:

"God, I believe You are good, and You are working in my waiting. I am Hope Full."

Use this strategy daily, weekly, or however you need. Let it be a living rhythm — a conversation between your heart and God's.

You don't have to pray perfectly. You just have to keep showing up.

He hears you. He is with you. And He is moving.

Stay Connected

If this story touched your heart or helped you in your own season of waiting, I would love to hear from you.

Whether you are walking through infertility, miscarriage, grief, or waiting on God for something else entirely — you are not alone. Your story matters. And it's still being written.

I invite you to reach out, share your testimony, or let me know how I can pray for you. I believe in the power of connection and community, and I would be honored to walk with you in faith.

⬦ Email: thewowmarriage@gmail.com

⬦ Social Media:
https://www.facebook.com/TheWowMarriage/
https://www.instagram.com/thewowmarriage/

Let's continue the conversation. Let's believe together. Let's stay Hope Full.

With love and faith,

Lisa Wood